Roadmap to the True Independence of Liberia

LIBERIA AND LIBERIAN FIRST

by Honorable Saywalla H. Dayrell

Dorrance Publishing Co
585 Alpha Drive
Suite 103
Pittsburgh, PA 15238
Visit our website at *www.dorrancebookstore.com*

ISBN: 979-8-89027-157-0
eISBN: 979-8-89027-655-1

Table of Contents

Roadmap to the True Independence of Liberia

LIBERIA AND LIBERIAN FIRST

Acknowledgements

I would like to pay tribute to my mother and father, who have already passed away. Their love and guidance provided the support that prepared me to write this book.

All the innocent Liberian people who lost their lives during the fourteen-year Civil War should be recognized for making the supreme sacrifice for our nation, including those who worked in the government at the time of the 1989 incursion. Some were killed by stray bullets, while others belonged to an enemy tribe and finally, some people were killed due to existing conflict before the war, they then became vulnerable to the advantage or gun carrier.

Many of our citizens stood firm to their principles of justice to protect the rights of all.

To these individuals and many others, I offer gratitude and respect. Your dedication and commitment to the well-being of Liberia and our people have inspired me to write this book. It is my hope and goal that Liberia will fulfill its promise to become a leading nation in Africa and around the globe.

Introduction
The Founding of Liberia: A Unique Beginning

The Republic of Liberia is black Africa's oldest independent nation, with independence declared 26 July 1847. Thus, unlike the rest of Africa, Liberia was never colonized, but was established as an independent country in the early nineteenth century. Populated by free people of color from the United States between 1820 and 1843, the early settlement of about 4,500 emigrants was reduced to less than 2,000 by the high mortality rate.

Located south of the Sahara Desert on the west coast of Africa bordering the Atlantic Ocean, Liberia's closest neighbors are Sierra Leone, Guinea, and La Cote d'Ivoire.

Liberia has an estimated population of 3.5 million: Approximately 95 percent are natives, 2.3 percent are Liberians of American descent, and the remaining 2.7 percent are Lebanese, Indigenous people, and other Africans residing and working in Liberia. Sixteen major ethnic groups are divided into three language families today:

- The Mande make up 47.2 percent of the population.
- The Kru comprise 41.3 percent.
- The West Atlantic represent 7.9 of the population.[3]

Approximately 48.3 percent of the population are traditionalists, 38.33 percent are Christians, 13.0 percent are Muslims, and 0.30% are Baha'i.[4]

Since its inception, Liberia has evolved as a land of rich cultures and traditions.[5] Liberia is also a land of "strongly entrenched and institutionalized secret societies"[6] involving every people group. The culture and tradition of the Liberian people are the connecting link enabling them to maintain their common identity and life. (https://lausanneworldpulse.com/themedarticles-php/1064/12-2008)

According to *Brittanica.com*, Pedro de Sintra, a Portuguese sailor, served as a European source for information about western Africa after visiting the Liberian coastal region in 1461. Later Portuguese travelers designed this area as the "Grain Coast" because of the valuable Melegueta pepper, which had become a premium trade item.

At the start of the nineteenth century, the abolitionist movement grew in popularity. The Liberian coast was identified as a relevant relocation of emancipated slaves:

> In 1818, two U.S. government agents and two officers of the American Colonization Society (founded 1816) visited the Grain Coast. After abortive attempts to establish settlements there, an agreement was signed in 1821 between the officers of the society and local African chiefs granting the society possession of Cape Mesurado. The first American freed slaves, led by members of the society, landed in 1822 on Providence Island at the mouth of the Mesurado River. They were followed shortly by Jehudi Ashmun, a white American, who became the real founder of Liberia. By the time Ashmun left in 1828, the territory had a government, a digest of laws for the settlers, and the beginnings of profitable foreign commerce. Other settlements were started along the St. John River, at Greenville, and at Harper. In 1839, Thomas Buchanan was appointed the first governor. On his death in 1841, he was succeeded by Joseph Jenkins Roberts, the

colony's first Black governor, who was born free in Virginia in 1809; Roberts enlarged the boundaries of the territory and improved economic conditions.

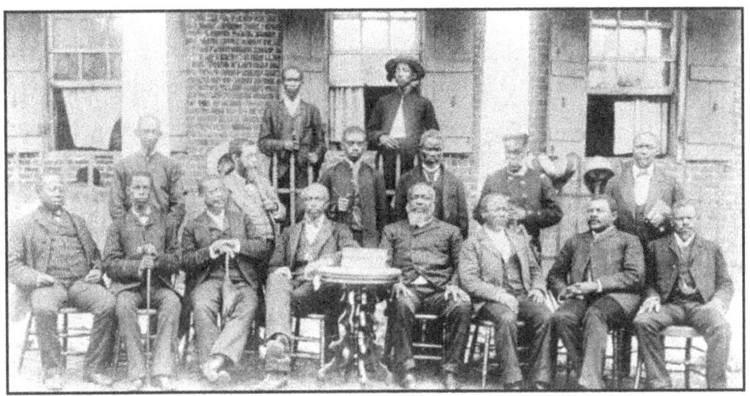

(Liberia - History | Britannica)

Later, the American Colonization Society suggested that Liberia should become independent of this organization. In 1847, Governor Roberts declared Liberia as a free republic 1847, and in 1848-56, independence was acknowledged by many nations, with the United States following suit in 1862.

Further development ensued:

> At the time independence was declared, a constitution based on that of the United States was drawn up. Roberts, who had been elected the first president of the republic, retained that office until 1856. During that period, the slave trade, theretofore illicitly continued from various nominally Liberian ports, was ended by the activity of the British and U.S. navies.
>
> In 1871, the first foreign loan was raised, being negotiated in London nominally for £100,000. The loan was unpopular, and still more unpopular was the new president, Edward J. Roye, who was deposed and imprisoned at Monrovia. Roberts was called back to the office. He served until 1876. (Liberia - History | Britannica)

Liberia's independence was not conflict-free. The nation clashed with French troops on Côte d'Ivoire and at Sierra Leone with the British. Treaties followed with the British in 1885 and with France in 1892. In 1904, Barbados-born President Arthur Barclay established a policy of tribal cooperation. In 1907, with the help of a London loan, reform initiatives were launched. Asserting and maintaining authority beyond twenty miles inland was not effective. In 1919, an agreement was implemented to give France 2,000 square miles of land claimed but not controlled by Liberia.

In 1909, U.S. President Theodore Roosevelt appointed a commission to investigate Liberia's political and economic conditions. A recommendation for financial reorganization resulted along with a loan of $1.7 million (U.S.), secured by customs revenue, arranged by an international consortium of bankers in 1912 with a receivership of customs to be administered by appointees of the British, French, and German governments, and a U.S. receiver-general. According to *Britannica.com*, "A frontier police officers of the U.S. Army organized force, with the result that Liberian authority was better maintained. However, ... this new regime was upset by World War I. Revenues dropped to one-fourth of their previous level, and the financial situation steadily deteriorated."

A major U.S. corporation, The Firestone Tire and Rubber Company, obtained "a concession of 1,000,000 acres (400,000 hectares) for a rubber plantation in 1926. At the same time, a loan was arranged through the Finance Corporation of America, a Firestone subsidiary. Using this private loan, the Liberian government consolidated and bonded all its external and internal debts and placed the country's finances on a stable basis. Administration of the customs and internal revenue was placed in the hands of a U.S. financial adviser. In 1952 the government was able to liquidate its foreign debt for the first time since accepting the English loan of 1871." (Liberia - History | Britannica)

An investigation by the League of Nations of forced labor and slavery in Liberia, involving the shipment of Africans to the Spanish plantations in Fernando Po, brought about the resignations of President Charles King and Vice President Allen Yancy and the election of Edwin Barclay to the presidency in 1931. Liberia appealed to the Council of the League of Nations for financial aid, and a commission of inquiry was established. The next three years were marked by unsuccessful attempts to work out a plan of assistance involving appointing foreign administrators, declaring a moratorium on the Firestone loan, and suspending diplomatic relations with Great Britain and the United States. After the League Council had finally withdrawn its plan of assistance, the Liberian government reached an agreement with Firestone along lines like the League's recommendations.

The promising start of this African nation hit several obstacles that led to unexpected consequences and the delay of achieving its original goals. The following chapters explore Liberia's dramatic history in greater detail with consideration of the problems that must be dealt as well as the country's promising future.

Chapter One
The American Colonization Society
(1816-1964)

The America Colonialization Society (ACS) was founded in 1817 by U.S. conservatives who were trying to help the free Black people and unenslaved people to escape discrimination and mistreatment by white Southerners and slaveholders as well as northern slavery supporters. The organization was acting in good faith to protect American Black people from harassment by providing a new home in the land of their ancestors.

But the hidden truth is that this relocation program caused the country of Liberia great harm from 1847 through 1980 and again up to 2023. Accordingly, Liberia can be referred to as the African country that has experienced the fastest economic growth without development. For example, Liberia's economy compares to Japan's in terms of GDP within the 1960s.

The Veracity Agenda

The ethos of the ACS at the time of the struggle to emancipate the Black people was not only good will, though any prudent person could reason to say that it was a good thing to escape slavery and return American Black people to another location where they could function as freeholders and become self-reliant. This ethos is evidenced by the fact that the Americo-Liberians were highly educated and refused to organize within Liberia but treated it as a home for all inhabitants. Today, Liberia does not depict the argument that Liberia and Japan were growing at the same GDP-rate at a particular time. (https://www.iexplore.com/articles/travel-guides/africa/liberia/history-and-culture)

From 1847 to 1980, Liberia was governed by the Americo-Liberian descendants of the original arrivals, a small minority of about five percent living in the country as more Indigenous ethnic groups migrated to the region. Four interactive developments formed the colony's history, all intertwined and reactive:

1. Relations between Indigenous tribes and the ruling colonists
2. The influence and intervention of the U.S. and other world powers
3. The economic strengths of natural resources
4. The evolution of industry

All these factors combined to influence Liberia's development and growth.

Integration between the colonists and the Indigenous people caused contention following the freed slaves' arrival, leading eventually to a revolution in 1980 that overthrew the Americo-Liberian government and ruling class. Tribal natives hated the lighter-skinned, mixed-ancestry migrants, their Christian beliefs, and supposed cultural superiority displayed in the Americanized way of life and architecture.

The veracity agenda is that at that time, ACS drafters were highly involved in money laundering, and the U.S. Government was cracking down on those associated with these illicit activities. So, the organization decided to relocate slaves belonging to them and create a new nation now called Liberia. In this newfound nation, they could impose their leader upon the residents by transplanting learned slaves, both men and women, a group that was far more educated than the

Indigenous people. Because they were educated, they could create a nation and take control of the leadership. That is why the ACS founded Liberia in 1822 and allowed themselves to declare independence 1847 as if giving birth to a nation.

Chapter Two
Joseph Jenkins Roberts
and the Educational Foundation

Joseph Jenkins Robert, Liberia's first president, was the face of the American Colonialization Society. By creating a national region, governance structure, and identity, Joseph J. Roberts served as the first head of state, fulfilling a successful mission for the conservative movement in the U.S. based on an interior motive:

A. To launder their dirty or stolen funds and recirculate the money to the U.S. as profit from business operations conducted in Liberia.

B. That motive was so strong that upon reaching the coast of Liberia, they could not document anything much about the local Indigenous or properly document important historical events like boundaries and resources such as mountains between Guinea and Liberia. Nor could they differentiate ethnic groups in Liberia that were like ethnic groups in neighboring regions. These and other important undocumented records that they should have done, but failed to do, has left a legacy of national doubts and problems.

C. Because of the founders' self-profiting motive, these individuals created an "open door policy in September 1953" that damaged the country further. Limited money entered Liberia and huge sums left without proper accountability.

D. That initial mindset has resonated with many Liberians both in public and private to keep that corrupt behavior alive. Liberia has been destroyed by that notion just as conservative motives have been passed down orally from generation to generation.

E. That conservative motive has been memorialized orally in a widespread manner and created a huge inequity for the distribution of wealth: "Don't tell anybody; it is just us and our foreign friends," as evidenced by the Liberia Mining Company in Bomi County, Tubmanburg. Firestone and many other Companies that have operated in our country and couple with the level of corruption we still observing.

F. The slaves were not aware of the ethos for which the conservatives behind the ACS authority decided to relocate them. The slaves thought it was actual freedom by choice. It was by choice, though, and that is why everyone was not forced to leave. But the ACS managed to encourage as many as possible to leave for so-called emancipation and personal freedom. They fought to get a few willing to enable them to create a nation and achieve their inner motive unknown to the free slaves by conducting business.

In Liberia, however, the freed slaves and the Indigenous experienced a series of confrontations that included land disputes, power limits, and many other conflicts that resulted in wars. The ACS and conservative supporters succeeded in establishing a government structure that was controlled by the Black people while the behind-the-scenes leaders executed their motive and allow free-slaves to colonize the territory by themselves because of taxes and to operate as a nation.

A few years after 1822, the Liberian government requested taxes from the British who were operating within its territories. The British wondered why they had been asked for taxes. Could the American operatives be acting on behalf of the U.S. because they lacked independence? The Liberian authority requested the American government through the ACS to help colonize them, but to no avail for fear of losing the power of "moral protectorate" over its territory now called Liberia.

The free Black people were able to declare independence in 1847 and started to function as a government to collect taxes within its borders. There were many limitations since the ACS refused to colonize the territory called Liberia; instead, it served as a catalyst. They still work with the Government from that time and up to the current 2023. Minerals and other resources still leave Liberia without proper accountability as though the conservatives were still alive with their bad motive that continued to descend.

The veracity agenda of the conservatives before creating Liberia is as compared to the motive for which the late American president emancipated the Black people in America. President Abraham Lincoln issued the Emancipation Proclamation on January 1, 1863, as the nation approached its third year of a bloody civil war. The Proclamation declared that "all persons held as slaves" within the rebellious states were, and henceforward, should be free.

This Proclamation was not issued from goodwill. The infirmity truth is that the President needed more men for recruitment to fight his war. He later realized that non-citizens could not be enlisted in the U.S military. He needed the Black people to fight alongside the white soldiers, so he emancipated and enlisted them. The Black people contributed immensely to Lincoln's civil war that resulted in victory that the nation and the entire world enjoys today.

Now, Liberia lacked the resources and means to defend itself and become completely autonomous. Over the next forty years, only about 13,000 Blacks from the United States migrated to Liberia. Some remained behind and accepted their status as second-class citizens. They felt that relocating to Liberia, an undeveloped country with an uncertain future, would be a precarious risk. Those that did migrate to the fledgling nation did so for entrepreneurial opportunities and Christian missions' outreach (FRONTLINE/WORLD. Liberia - No More War. Liberia's Historic Ties to America | PBS).

But who were the main beneficiaries of this initiative?

The U.S. government had established the boundaries and objectives for Liberia for its own purposes. The settlement was intended to help the government monitor the illicit slave commerce that shipped Indigenous Black people from western Africa across the Atlantic Ocean to North America for free labor. The captive slaves that were reclaimed on the high seas were brought back by the British to Sierra Leone while the French unloaded their human cargo in Gabon. In 1824, the United States had designated the region of Liberia as the unloading site for its returned natives or American slaves to be governed by the American Colonization Society without oversight or control by U.S. authorities.

As the newly formed nation of Liberia struggled to define itself and become independent of foreign influences. In 1847, the country issued a declaration of freedom from the ACS. The first Black governor of Liberia under the auspices of the American Colonization Society since 1841 was duly elected as the president of the independent nation in 1841. However, in the United States, political upheaval over the issue of slavery prevented Joseph Jenkins Roberts from being acknowledged as the official government leader of Liberia until 1862.

Freed Black people were the prominent social group in Liberia. Many had arrived in the nation with possessions and material wealth, and they held positions of authority and power as the "true Whig party" until the late twentieth century. Unwanted slaves from the U.S. occupied a lower social tier. The region's natives were not included in the government structure and remained outcasts assigned basic labor work by the Americo-Liberians and were treated as lower-class citizens. Just a fraction of the original American Black descendants are part of the current twenty-first century population.

Globally, the 1800s introduced an era of turbulent change. With the evolution of the Industrial Revolution of the late eighteenth century, cottage industries were replaced by factories and mass production. Individual or family specialties were overtaken by the nascent origins of assembly line processes. Many family farms and businesses went out of business, and their lands were sold as they moved into urban areas. Education rates began to rise and expanded across the world's population as more people learned to read and became literate, especially in Europe and America.

Urbanization brought new challenges and problems, such as a decline in morality (except for Victorian England) and rising crime in slum areas of cities. Christian church outreach in the grew and fostered missionary programs that traveled to distant lands to reach Indigenous or uneducated populations as well as those that practiced a different religious faith. The growth of European nationalism and the explosion of simmering contentious issues like slavery led to civil conflicts, regional battles, and international wars. The continued growth of liberalism and self-determination that had led to wars of independence in the eighteenth century contributed to some of these residual issues and raised questions of human rights, Christian values, and secular authority.

Joseph Jenkins Roberts was born on March 15, 1809, to Amelia Roberts who was known to be intelligent, morally upright, and hardworking. Her husband, Joseph's stepfather, was a free Black person of good reputation. Of seven children, Henry became a doctor, and John served as a Bishop of Liberia's Methodist Church. Their brother Joseph became the first President of Liberia, Africa's first republic. Although Black people often lacked the means to buy property, James got involved with the transportation business and owned several flatboats used to move products to various locations. Biography – Joseph Jenkin Roberts Educational Foundation (jjref.org)

Well educated, Joseph Jenkins Roberts also received Liberia's mandatory skill training that prepared youth for jobs as tailors, electricians, or carpenters, among others. Further, Joseph's stepfather James taught him how to conduct business. Subsequently, Joseph became an apprentice at a barber shop owned by the Reverend William N. Colson and was encouraged to read from the Reverend's personal library. More responsibility came Joseph's way when his stepfather passed away, leaving two houses, some boats, and other property as well as land. Joseph helped his mother manage these assets and guide the younger children. Possibly because of their material resources, the family moved to Liberia to enjoy greater social freedom and respect.

They boarded a ship named *the Harriet* on February 9, 1829, and reached Liberia on March 24. After their arrival, they came down with malaria, but everyone in the family survived. Although hardships faced Amelia and her children as they settled into their new homeland, she did not regret her decision and had no desire to return to the United States.

Joseph partnered with long-time family friend, Reverend Colson of Virginia, to open a trading company that sold goods between Liberia and the United States. Joseph's challenging work and sound business ethics impressed the Americans as well as the Liberians. Despite his commercial success, Joseph grew concerned about the wellbeing of the Liberian Commonwealth. Learning all he could from those around him as well as through his community interactions, Joseph Jenkins Roberts' knowledge and influence increased. In 1833, he was elected as High Sheriff of Liberia to oversee elections and work with the Indigenous residents to manage conflicts within their tribes and with the immigrants from America.

Proving himself a competent leader, J. J. Roberts was appointed as Lieutenant-Governor. His duties teamed him with Governor Thomas Buchanan, who was the brother of U.S. President James Buchanan. Two of the most pressing issues were the ongoing slave trade as Liberian citizens cooperated with slave traders from Europe to sell family members and other African tribal members. A second issue was inducing the American settlers and the Indigenous people to cooperate and live side by side harmoniously, aided by diplomacy with violence only as needed.

Governor Buchanan died on September 3, 1841, and the Board of Directors of the American Colonization Society (ACS) appointed

Roberts as Buchanan's successor. Joseph's leadership ability was acknowledged by all in his belief that Liberia could become a vibrant nation. His goals were for the country's population to live in a free and just democracy.

Commercial trade between the U.S. and Liberia improved through the government owned Chesapeake Company and the Liberia Trading Company. Still, problems surfaced that Roberts was determined to resolve, as discussed in the previous chapter. ETHNIC Group leaders were invited to join Liberia's Commonwealth, and many agreed. The new settlers were able to form colonies, as they called them. But opponents to this plan would attack the settlements and cause upheaval.

The new Governor wanted to eliminate Liberia's slave trade. The second major concern of Governor Roberts was the total abolition of the slave trade in Liberia and replace it with a compensation program. With the support of the American and British governments, Roberts eventually eradicated slavery in Liberia.

Education was his third objective. Since there were no colleges or universities at that time, he developed an apprenticeship program to teach everyone an occupation that would enable them to earn income. In tandem with that initiative, Governor Roberts fostered missionary ventures with schools. Eventually, Liberia College was established and later became the University of Liberia. Of special interest was the education of female children to provide a means of support and skills for family management.

All his life, Roberts believed in the potential for Black people. Although he had heard as a youth the complaints that Blacks were backward, lazy, and inferior, in Liberia he witnessed firsthand that the Indigenous Liberians disproved those stereotypes. However, he did believe that the Indigenous tribes did not know the Christian God and his offer of salvation. He did not realize that the regional tribal life included a diverse culture with inherent systems of religion, politics, and economics. Making Liberia a Christian nation was one of his life-long goals.

Thus, Christianity was not forced on the Liberian natives. Over time, with cultural exchanges and interactions, the tribal chiefs sought out Christianity and American education for the inhabitants. Biography – Joseph Jenkin Roberts Educational Foundation (jjref.org)

It didn't take long for Governor Roberts to see that national independence was becoming imperative for Liberia's growth and prosperity.

> On January 18, 1844, the American Colonization Society corresponded with the leaders of the Commonwealth and told them, "the time had arrived when it was expedient for the people of the Commonwealth of Liberia to take into their own hands the whole work of self-government, including the management of all their foreign relations." Biography – Joseph Jenkin Roberts Educational Foundation (jjref.org)

The Commonwealth agreed to hold a referendum to assess the residents' will. The people voted for independence. Boston lawyer, Simon Greenleaf, prepared a Constitution like that of the U.S. Roberts convened a Constitutional Assembly with delegates from around the region.

On July 26, 1847, "prayers of thanksgiving and praises to God and moments of jubilation" welcomed Liberia's declaration of independence. On the first Tuesday in October of 1847, Roberts was elected over opponent Samuel Benedict to become the first President of the Republic of Liberia. Biography – Joseph Jenkin Roberts Educational Foundation (jjref.org)

At this point, President Joseph J. Roberts felt that he should visit Europe to help Liberia establish an international niche and identity. Before he could embark on this visit, the British Foreign Minister, Lord Palmerston, recommended to his government that Liberia be recognized and its flag be treated "as that of an independent state." Biography – Joseph Jenkin Roberts Educational Foundation (jjref.org)

In Great Britain, President Roberts met with Queen Victoria at a state reception on her royal yacht. The Foreign Minister and Roberts formalized an Accord of recognition and friendship between the two nations.

From Britain, President Roberts traveled to France where Napoleon III gave him a formal reception. The French Foreign Office affirmed that Liberia's petition for recognition would receive full consideration.

Then, President Roberts made a trip to Belgium where Leopold, I governed. Discussions ensued with promises that followed indicating that Liberia in time would be recognized. A similar response was given in the Netherlands and Prussia.

The Liberian President came home with the sense that Liberia was going to be recognized by the major European countries. To shore up these allegiances, he returned to Europe in 1851 and received additional assurances from France, Brazil, and Prussia.

In 1854, Roberts made a third trip to Europe to discuss trade and commerce with the first minting of Liberia coins. Exports increased to $1 million (about $800,000.00). Even after the President's term ended, Roberts's efforts are acknowledged as essential to Liberia's recognition as an independent nation by several European powers between 1858 and 1866.

Agricultural production and education remained high priorities. Roberts initiated the purchase of more land to extend the country's boundaries. His overarching dream was for all Liberian citizens to embrace their independence and assume control of their future in support of "liberty and equal rights." Biography – Joseph Jenkin Roberts Educational Foundation (jjref.org)

President Roberts served six terms in office. In his later years as President, he was labeled a "mulatto" and thus not of full Black heritage for ruling Liberia, a national for Black people and the Indigenous people. Following his retirement, he held the position of Professor and President of Liberia College. His life was characterized by his Christian faith and trusted in God's providence for the people of Liberia and their quest for freedom.

Following an illness, Joseph J. Roberts died on February 24, 1876. His homegoing service was held at the First United Methodist Church on Ashmun Street.

> A 30-day mourning period was declared, and tributes came from all over the United States and Europe. Historian C. Abayomi Cassell described Roberts as "Liberia's Son, a patriot and founder whose wisdom and foresight are unparalleled in the history of the country he love." (Cassell 29)

President Roberts left a legacy for Liberia in his Will. He bequeathed property and funds to establish a "perpetual foundation" … for the increasing of educational facilities of the country." (Biography – Joseph Jenkin Roberts Educational Foundation (jjref.org))

Joseph J. Roberts believed in the dream for Liberia to become an independent nation that would attract international respect and commerce. He devoted much of his adult life to making that dream come true.

However, a peaceful and successful future for Liberia was not yet assured.

Chapter Three
The Politization of Liberia

In 1817, the America Colonization Society (ACS) was founded by Conservatives in the U.S. Established to benefit both freed American slaves and the Indigenous population of the West African region, the ACS caused great harm to the organic development of Liberia. From 1847 up to 1980 and then forward to 2023, Liberia became known as the fastest-growing African nation without development. In the 1960s, its economy was often compared to that of Japan with respect to GDP.

Hidden Agenda

The conservative movement that led to the founding of Liberia as a homeland for freed American slaves was not just an act of good will. Any prudent person will readily support institutionalized slavery and return the victims and their descendants to their region of origin or establish another area as a residential territory that would enable the former slaves to become self-reliant. Many of the Americo-Liberians were highly educated and refused to organize Liberia as a nation for all inhabitants. (https://www.iexplore.com/articles/travel-guides/africa/liberia/history-and-culture)

Between 1847 and 1980, Liberia was governed by descendants of the original arrivals, which was a small minority of about five percent despite the arrival of Indigenous ethnic groups who had migrated to the region. This led to conflicts and clashes that remained mostly steady or grew as the years passed. Although mentioned earlier in this book, they are worth reviewing again as we move forward.

- Troubled relations ensued between Indigenous tribes and the ruling colonists. (Tribesmen resented the lighter-skinned, mixed-ancestry migrants with their Christian religion and suggestions of cultural superiority as evidenced in the American architecture and cultural practices. However, the ACS founders became involved in money laundering, causing the U.S. government to send the slaves of these offenders to the newly organized nation, Liberia. Educated slaves were shipped to Liberia to create a new government and assume leadership under the tacit supervision of American Conservatives. In 1847, the Liberia settlement declared independence as discussed in earlier chapters.

- Joseph Jenkins Roberts, the first Liberian President, was also the head of the ACS. He was able to coordinate the objectives of the founding Conservatives with those of the new young nation to "clean" the "dirty" monetary deals so that the business ventures in Liberia sent profits back to the United States.

- Intent on fulfilling this major goal, the original settlers and subsequent arrivals failed to make adequate records about or for the Indigenous local tribes. Geophysical resources like the mountains between Guinea and Liberia were left uncharted. There was no effort to coordinate objectives with the area tribes and nearby neighbors, which led to ongoing conflicts and problems.

- In September 1953, an "open door policy" was established that damaged Liberia even more. Lower amounts of money entered the country while enormous amounts left without adequate accountability.

- Although these unwanted activities were clandestine or small scale at first, the practices increased. Liberia has been destroyed by corrupt policies just as the conservative culture has been orally but powerfully handed down from one generation to another.
- The de facto government leaders created a significant inequality for the sharing of wealth that was downplayed to or hidden from the public. Foreign corporations like Firestone and the Liberia Mining Company in Tubmanburg represent companies operating in Liberia and have contributed to a reputation for corruption that Liberians are still dealing with.

Some of these events and processes evolved over generations while others are recent. Combined, they have taken a detrimental toll on Liberia's economic and social development that continues to be felt today.

The Push for Real Independence

The slaves were unaware of the motive behind the ACS push to relocate freed American slaves to the western coast of Africa. Most slaves thought it was actual freedom by choice.

Not everyone was forced to leave, but the ACS persuaded as many as possible to migrate for freedom. The founders fought for a few willing to allow them to establish a nation to achieve their inner motive by conducting money laundry activities, of which the slaves were unaware. While in Liberia, the free-slaves and the Indigenous had series of confrontation like land disputes, power limits, many other things that resulted into wars. The ACS and conservatives were able to establish government control by the Black people while they pursued their motives.

A few years after 1822, the Liberian government requested taxes from the British entities that were operating within its territories. The British questioned why they were asked for taxes; could the Liberian government be acting on behalf of the Americans because Liberia did not have independence? The free Black people were able to declare independence in 1847 and started to operate as a government to collect taxes within its borders. They met with many limitations since the ACS refused to colonize the country of Liberia because of their original motive and intent. They have still worked with the Government since then and continue through the present. Yet, minerals leave Liberia as though the motive were still active. Liberian resources continue to be taken from the country without proper accountability or record-keeping.

The hidden motive that the conservatives had before creating Liberia can be compared to the ulterior motive for which the late American President emancipated the Black people in America. President Abraham Lincoln issued the Emancipation Proclamation on January 1, 1863, as the nation approached its third year of bloody civil war. The Proclamation declared that "all persons held as slaves" within the rebellious states are, and henceforward shall be free.

This Proclamation was not born out of goodwill. The hidden truth is that President Lincoln needed more soldiers for recruitment to fight his war. He later realized that non-citizens cannot be enlisted into national military service. He needed the Black people to help fight alongside his men, so he emancipated them and enlisted them as soldiers. The black recruits contributed immensely to Lincoln's civil war that resulted into a victory the entire world enjoys today.

What can be seen in the nineteenth century is that U.S. initiatives for mass-changing the status and rights of Black residents typically came from hidden motives that could be self-seeking.

Chapter Four
Liberia's Religions

Most people are familiar with the world's main religions, including Judaism, Christianity, Islam, Hinduism, and Buddhism, among others. Some of these religions were brought to Africa by traders, explorers, armies, missionaries, and settlers. Certain faiths took root in parts of Africa while others had negligible effect on the Indigenous residents of the continent. With the establishment and evolution of numerous countries on the continent, religion is one of the many cultural and social aspects that remain a strong influence on the residents and their respective regions.

Traditional Religion

Among African natives, a common religious faith is called "traditional religion." It was practiced among the Indigenous people according to the various tribes' beliefs and customs. Some worshipped snakes, others idolized bodies of water like a creek or waterfall, and some worshipped unseen aliens from outer space. There were numerous manifestations of Traditional Religion that all pointed to a series of gods or a supreme deity. Practitioners of these belief systems shared the sense of belonging to a god or several gods, some on a higher level of existence, with others in a lower category than humans. Harvest rituals were frequently dedicated to their designation of one or more deities in gratitude for the current harvest and in petition for the next year's crops. This ancient religious system was practiced long before the arrival of Middle Eastern religions like Christianity and Islam through white travelers and pioneers.

The emphasis here is to distinguish the religions practiced by our natives originally as there was nothing like Islam or Christianity existing in Liberia until the past few centuries with the coming of Christian missionaries and Islamic jihad. In general, traditional religions in Africa were shared and preserved through the oral traditions of song, stories, and celebrations rather than through written scriptures.

Widespread Religious Influences

Africa's 54 nations (and a few other associated territories) practice many diverse religions. However, many of these belief systems attempt to coordinate the natural world, or experiential reality, with supernatural events that cannot be readily explained through human knowledge. Living in harmony with the vast nature reserves and ecosystems of mountains, deserts, rivers, and plains along with native animal species is another common thread found in many traditional religions of the African people.

Ancestor worship is another characteristic of traditional African religion. Rituals commemorating deceased loved ones are an important part of religious culture. Many Africans believe that their long-ago ancestors communicate with them and influence their behavior in positive ways. Most dead spirits are viewed as benign or beneficial. Spirits are rarely malevolent beyond causing a minor disturbance, like illness or losing something of value, to someone with whom they did not have a good relationship with while alive. Animism, a belief in the interactive connectedness between humans and the spirit world, is an important attribute of traditional religion in Africa.

Religious leaders, sometimes referred to in the western vernacular as "witch doctors" or "priests," play a key role in tribal society. They reinforce the spiritual framework of the community by leading religious ceremonies and festivals. These shaman-like figures undergo extensive training to learn how to heal with natural herbs as well as use mental powers to "divine" unknown information, such as finding a lost animal or determining the cause of a spreading illness.

Combining and Confusing Religions

Over many centuries, other religions entered African regions through the means mentioned above. In particular, the three Abrahamic faiths – Judaism, Christianity, and Islam – forged strong bonds with African communities where many Indigenous ethnic groups adopted their teachings and practiced that faith. But these three religions also adapted to these new locales and societies by accepting new rites and customs as forms of worship. African foods, clothing, and beliefs were integrated into the original Jewish, Christian, and Islamic religions so that the version practiced in Africa was more of a blend of diverse cultures and religions. The way these faiths were and continue to be practiced in some areas resembles more of a hybrid variant of the Abrahamic faiths. Each successive generation added its own beliefs and practices to the evolutionary religious system that had adapted to a specific region.

Christians and Muslims came to Africa in part to proselytize the Indigenous residents, sometimes peacefully and other times forcefully. To a large degree, they were successful, although sometimes their methods had insidious results. Other religious rites and beliefs may have also filtered into the Africans' traditional religion along with the Abrahamic faiths, such as India's Dravidian folk religion.

Christianity and Islam maintain dedicated support bases in Africa, according to Religion Media Centre:

> The US research organization for the study of religion and public life has estimated that Africa has the world's third largest Catholic population and fast-growing Pentecostal churches. It says that by 2050, the number of Christians in Africa will double, meaning that 40% of the world's Christian population will live in sub-Saharan Africa.

But the long-range influence of these world faiths on the Indigenous residents of Africa is questionable. Because of the establishment of Islam, for example, its crafters were very smart to easily win over our native inhabitants. They instituted a combination of religious ideals and practices in establishing Islam. The Islamic settlers adopted many practices of the traditional religion that was practiced by natives, such as using their garment, caps, and jewelries. Islamist "recruiters" adopted African rituals like the cutting of sand for telling the future, adopting certain names, travel by camels, and architectural styles. While appropriating many traditional and cultural aspects of religious practice from the native people, they refused to conform to worshipping snakes or other natural elements as well as aliens or other supernatural figures.

Some Indigenous inhabitants are confused about religious beliefs and systems because when history mentions a specific name or describes a strict dress code or a practice such as telling the future by "cutting sand," it is assumed that Islam existed in that part of Liberia because those attributes have been adopted. The reality is that the religious systems merged in many ways to render a new and distinctive faith-based system of worship in the country and surrounding areas as a blend of the traditional African religion with the subsequent Middle Eastern faiths.

It was also easy for our traditional people to transition to Islam since some of the practices were similar to their traditional system of religious worship as they were introduced to two dominant practices other them their own, according to Liberia's Religious Institutions:

Most Muslims belong to two distinct ethnic groups, the Mandingo—who are widely distributed—and the Vai, who live mostly in western areas.

Organized Christianity reached Liberia in the 19th century with the arrival of freed slaves from the United States. Missionaries of various Protestant denominations started arriving in the 1820s, eventually forming what became one of the highest per capita missionary populations in the world. The first permanent Catholic mission in the country was established in the early 1900s. A Liberian Council of Churches composed of Lutheran, Episcopal, Methodist, and other similar groups now exists, and an evangelical association of churches and missions has operated on and off since 1966. Though religious violence in Liberia is uncommon, tensions between Christians and Muslims have escalated in the past. In October 2004, approximately twenty-five people were killed, and several churches and mosques were destroyed in Monrovia during clashes between Christians of several ethnic groups and Mandingo Muslims.

The Liberian Constitution provides religious freedom for all inhabitants, and in practice, the government respects minority religious groups. According to a 2013 document published by the U.S. Department of State, the Liberian government does not discriminate based on religious affiliation, belief, or worship. Although there is no state religion in the country, government ceremonies commonly begin and end with prayers or hymns, the majority of which are Christian, though some are Muslim. Most private schools in Liberia are operated by churches or missions. Most receive government funding, though non-religious schools are also subsidized. Religious education is available as an elective but not required in public schools.

Religious organizations manage social welfare institutions, often coordinated with international aid agencies. Some Liberian leaders attribute the Ebola crisis in West Africa to "immoral acts." In August 2014, Liberia's Council of Churches agreed, "God is angry with Liberia," and urged Liberians to seek forgiveness for corruption and immorality by staying indoors and fasting for three days.

Liberians comprise ethnic groups that practiced traditional religion within their respective ways before the coming of Christianity and Islam. People from most Liberian ethnic groups have turned away from their traditional practices because of the adopted religions, Christianity, and Islam. Shifting to a monotheistic faith was a substantial change for people who had worshipped numerous deities in the traditional African religion. The single biggest difference between traditional religion and Islam is that Islam refused to adopt the natural aspect of worshipping rocks, snakes, mountains, and other nature-associated elements.

We need to begin to embrace our traditional cultures, and each tribe needs to display traditional items that help them survive before the coming of foreign religions that changed our lives. We need to avoid tribal and religious conflict and work together to rebuild our nation.

Traditional Religion + Christianity + Islam

The Evolution of Liberian religion:

- Traditional people
- Freed slaves
- Foreign missionaries and conquerors

Christianity can be summarized as in the Bible as found in Matthew 22:37-40: "Love God above all things and love your neighbor as yourself."

Islam is based on Five Pillars, which are the core beliefs and practices stemming from the Profession of Faith, called the Shahada: "There is no god but God, and Muhammad is the Messenger of God."

Despite these differences and contentions, we must avoid religious hatred and discrimination. Instead, we must build our nation as the only home that we will have forever by learning to respect our differences and celebrate our commonalities.

My point is to remind us to collectively display our traditional culture that made us unique regardless of our individual choice to adopt a second religion.

Chapter Five
Liberia's Economic Challenges

Liberia faces many problems that affect daily life and long-term productivity. Poverty, lack of education, and foreign imports continue to prevent the country from becoming stable and moving forward toward future prosperity.

Causes of Civil War in Liberia

The underlying causes that led to civil war within our borders created conditions that destroyed our cultures, albeit unrecognized by ourselves. Openly, we declare the below reasons for starting the war because we want for the loss of life and resources to make sense and to appear justified to the world. If the reasons below are credible, then did we achieved our objectives?

Since its early days, our country has regressed in terms of development, infrastructure, education, technology, and agriculture, among other aspects of our culture. Our inconsistent approach to developing and maintaining our nation and ourselves in exchange for short-term gains suggests that personal greed at the expense of our nation has led to the Civic War. This greediness stems from the following shortfalls:

Failure to invest in human capital:

a) Government's failure to distribute wealth/resources equally to all citizens.
b) The economy's lack of job opportunity for all tribes/citizens.
c) Failure of human resource development for citizens.

Failure to effectively manage land disputes:

1. The Wasted Years began in 1822 and continue to the present. Unless an improvement is made by a responsible government to change the course of history in Liberia to favor of its citizens.
2. Liberia was founded in 1822 and gained independence in 1847. Civil War broke up the country in December 1989 and ended in 2003 but yielded nothing due to personal greed. Alleged Contributors include Ellen J. Sirleaf, Charles Taylor, Amos Sawyer, Roosevelt Johnson, A. G. V. Kromah, Prince Johnson, and many other politicians and Warlords.
3. Since 1822, Liberia has never progressed under any President who has demonstrated unselfish "love of country," instead emphasizing love for oneself by gathering wealth for future generations disregarding Liberia growth and prosperity. Most Government functions was performed within private building from corrupt owners who played major roles within the Liberian Politics since 1822. This can visually be proving by Ministry of Finance and other Ministries today to kept earning from government by rental agreement and such will be inherited by their children's children. George Weah recently created income string for his generational line by building 49 huge buildings that could possibly serve as a rental property when need be. There will be a need when no government does the right thing regarding LOVE FOR COUNTRY!!!!

Liberia's Economic Issues

In 2019, a report was published by the Liberian Economy Group (LEG) titled "Liberia's Economic Problems: Longstanding and Widespread Poverty, Unbearably High Foreign exchange rate" [sic]. The report indicated the 1989 to 2003 Civil War in Liberia with 300,000 casualties as well as numerous injured persons that affected ten percent of Liberia's population. It pointed out that Ellen Johnson Sir Leaf had declared corruption to be a leading cause of Liberia's problems in the 2015 State of the Nation Address. Despite published intent by various entities to eradicate poverty, the situation has not improved. In fact, the economy has worsened as evidenced in the deterioration of the Liberian dollar (LD) from LD130 to U.S. one dollar (USD) as of December 2018 to LD215 to USD1 in September 2019 (Liberia's Economic Problems: The Longstanding and Widespread Poverty, Unbearably High Foreign exchange rate (theperspective.org).

The alarming rise in the cost-of-living conditions, including food, housing, and medical care, has incited the population's anger, that, over time, has led to violence. From this situation, the **Liberian Economy Group (LEG),** numbering seven scientist members, formed to respectfully define and address the serious issues that are hindering the country's stability, security, and success.

LEG has identified "longstanding and widespread poverty" making Liberia the second poorest country in Africa and fourth poorest in the world as the root problem. Two thirds of children are not in school, which UNICEF (UNICEF Annual Report) has rated as the world's worst record.

In addition, the climbing foreign exchange rate between Liberia and the United States dollar has severely damaged the Liberian economy.

The example of a national crisis shows how the nation's population can address its own problems. Liberia's Ebola epidemic motivated people to work together to discover the source of the outbreak and solve it. Solidarity and shared commitment resolved the problem.

LEG refers to a publication by the late Veteran Journalist Stanton Peabody in the *Daily Observer* newspaper wherein he stated that the "main problem of Liberia is the Over-Americanization" of the country. Trying to solve Liberia's problems by utilizing America's cultural values rather than Liberian cultural values, he believed, led to a decline in the Liberians' living conditions. Developing a taste for American vs. Liberian products not only meant that Liberians paid higher prices for imported U.S. goods but also that Liberia's raw materials were exported rather than used in-country to benefit its people, the economy, and the culture. Liberia's issues cannot be resolved using American and European tactics. LEG claims that the most effective response to this problem is to raise awareness in all Liberian sectors, including families, communities, schools, religious organizations, government, and business.

Proposed Actions

1. Credible leaders should inform the people of Liberia about the problems associated with poverty and explore action steps for addressing these issues.
2. Cultural entities that include families, communities, civil society, and others can organize meetings and gathering events to share information and discuss strategies.
3. The Rule of Law should be emphasized as applied in Liberia's Constitution using Liberian languages and English as well as Standard English. The people can institute change through the Rule of Law.
    A. The Electoral System should be revised to operate according to Liberia's Constitution and ensure fair elections to elect leaders of integrity with a history of working on behalf of the nation's interests. Effective gov-

ernance will wipe out widespread corruption and reduce nationwide poverty to improve residents' living conditions.

B. The Value Addition approach should be used to increase the value of human resources via education. The population can become educated and commit to making choices that will improve Liberia for everyone. Western history and culture should not be the focus in education or government as this detracts from targeting Liberia's issues using Liberian strategies. Adding value to foreign nations should end, and manufacturing in Liberia should add value to the country's raw materials.

C. Local Purchasing should be practiced rather than importing foreign goods. Commercial bank loans should be issued primarily to Liberia's business enterprises instead of overseas businesses.

D. Utilize the Savings Generation Method. Savings should be generated privately and publicly to provide financing for entities that foreigners are handling.

E. Liberian goods should be favored over foreign goods. LEG estimates that savings of USD100,000,000 can be achieved.

F. Cost Adjustments can increase government savings and reduce spending based on the 2019-2020 National Budget and GOL budgets over the next four years from that time.

The recommendations of LEG include salary adjustments for government leaders from the President to each legislator. Foreign travel would be limited to the President or his Designate and the Foreign Minister "with entourage of seven and two, respectively" for travel to GOL missions. Other travel limits are also recommended for other government leaders. Official vehicles would be limited to the President, Vice President, and Foreign Minister.

In addition, the GOL should purchase only from Liberian businesses. Salaries would be paid in Liberian dollars without additional "perks" except for those mentioned previously.

These and other changes could result in savings of $345,000,000. Further, the Assets Recovery Committee reported that "total savings could be increased by at least USD2,000,000,000 ($2 billion USD).

The LEG report includes a budget for equipment to clear land in all Liberia counties, hiring Liberian contractors to make farm-to-market roads, buying Liberian-made chairs and desks for public schools, hiring Liberians to build and renovate public schools, regularizing the salaries of teachers and health workers, providing financial support and training for moving GOL employees to private sector income generation situations, establishing road construction and maintenance projects, and promoting sensitization and action on sanitation and climate change.

Finally, the LEG report indicates that the Liberian dollar will improve and reduce poverty. Buying Liberian products with Liberian money instead of using U.S. currency to buy U.S.-made products will help to heal Liberia's economy. Here's a summary of a Statement at the Senate Confirmation Hearing by the former Executive Governor of the Central Bank of Liberia, Nathaniel Patray:

> LD16 billion (sixteen billion Liberian dollars) were imported by the GOL into Liberia between 2016 and 2018, but by July 2018, **LD15, 242,000,000** (fifteen billion, two hundred and forty-two billion Liberian dollars) were outside of the banking system in Liberia. Therefore, to get the United States dollar, more Liberian dollars must be used, and with the use of more Liberian dollars, the foreign rate of exchange will continue to go up. To get the foreign exchange rate to go down, Liberians will have to prefer the Liberian dollar to the United States dollar. Such preference takes place when raw materials in Liberia are produced mainly for local production and consumption, through manufacturing. Liberians must produce what they can produce and stop importing

products that they can produce. Liberians must buy from Liberian owned businesses, paying in Liberian dollars. The Government must pay salaries in Liberian dollars and collect taxes in Liberian dollars. When Liberia adds value to the production of Liberia's raw materials, through manufacturing, and export the manufactured products, after attending to local consumption, then we get needed foreign exchange to import products that we cannot produce. When Liberia imports only those products that we cannot produce, at his time, while concentrating on local production and consumption of products from Liberian businesses, the Liberian dollar gets stronger, local prices become bearable and mass poverty elimination moves towards reality. (Liberia's Economic Problems: The Longstanding and Widespread Poverty, Unbearably High Foreign exchange rate (theperspective.org))

When government leaders, business enterprises, and the people of Liberia work together, they can overcome these economic challenges to escape the chronic hardships of illiteracy, conflict, and poverty. The dissemination of knowledge is the first step to informing everyone about the nature of these issues and the best ways of overcoming our difficulties to become a unified nation thriving on its own resources without interference from or competition with foreign powers.

Chapter Six
Contextual Culture Realities

Liberia's population is diverse and complex for several reasons. The country's inception as a homeland for freed American slaves brought Black people born and raised in U.S. slavery back to their African roots. However, many freed slaves were multiracial people with mixed racial or ethnic identity. Some were highly educated and migrated to Liberia to start a business.

With the establishment of Liberia's borders and an influx of immigrants from the West, regional Indigenous people settled in the area as well. These migrants came from various ethnic groups with different languages, religions, and traditions that diversified Liberia's population and culture. According to Britannica.com, those residing in Liberia represent three major groups:

> The people of Liberia are classified into three major groups: the indigenous people, who are in the majority and who migrated from the western Sudan in the late Middle Ages; Black immigrants from the United States (known historically as Americo-Liberians) and the West Indies; and other Black immigrants from neighbouring western African states who came during the anti-slave-trade campaign and European colonial rule. The Americo-Liberians are most strongly associated with founding Liberia. Most of them migrated to Liberia between 1820 and 1865;

continued migration has been intermittent. Americo-Liberians controlled the government until a military coup in 1980.

Liberia: Ethnic composition

Liberia's Indigenous ethnicities may be classified into three linguistic groups, all belonging to the Niger-Congo language family: the Mande, Kwa, and Mel (southern Atlantic). The Mande are located in the northwest and central regions of Liberia and also in Senegal, Mali, Guinea, and Sierra Leone. Prominent among them are the Vai, who invented their own alphabet and who, in addition, use Arabic and English; the Kpelle, the largest Mande group, who are also found in Guinea; Loma (also found in Guinea); Ngbandi; Dan (Gio); Mano; Mende; and Malinke. Kwa-speaking peoples include the Bassa, the largest group in this category and the largest ethnic group in Monrovia; the Kru and Grebo, who were among the earliest converts to Christianity; the De; Belleh (Belle); and Krahn. The Kwa-speaking group occupies the southern half of the country. The Mel group includes the Gola and Kisi, who are also found in Sierra Leone and are known to be the oldest inhabitants of Liberia. These people live in the north and in the coastal region of the northwest. (Liberia - People | Britannica)

Population

As of 2022, Liberia's population is estimated to be 5,358,483 with an estimated growth rate of 2.73 percent. Nearly half are teens or young adults due to the devastating losses from civil wars and an Ebola outbreak that killed many parents. Although the official language is English, there are approximately twenty Indigenous languages commonly spoken in the country. Christianity is the main religion, but Islam and other major world faiths are practiced by some Liberians and protected by the government's freedom of religion policy.

The capital city of Liberia is Monrovia, named for U.S. President James Monroe. President Monroe supported the plan for establishing an independent colony on Africa's western coast for American slaves who had been emancipated while maintaining the institution of slavery in the United States. The designated site was a region near Cape Mesurado and the mouth of the Mesurado River in an area called Ducor. It had existed for a long time before this as a trade crossroads. Settlers included farmers, fishers, and traders of different ethnicities, including the Bassa, Dey, Gola, and Vai people. The male life expectancy is about 57 years while the female's is about 60 years and is one of the lowest in the world, like that of other sub-Saharan African nations.

The American Colonization Society transported a ship of freed African American settlers in West Africa that arrived at Sherbro Island in territory today called Sierra Leone (Monrovia - Wikipedia). The ex-slaves brought with them vestiges of American life, including architecture, foods, and customs they had learned and practiced as slaves.

> There are more than 2,000 villages, the majority of which are concentrated in central Liberia, in the northwest, and in the coastal region near Monrovia. The predominantly forested regions of south-central and northern Liberia have remained sparsely populated. There is a strong rural-to-urban movement, especially to Monrovia. Other destinations include enclaves around rubber plantations and mines. The trend toward urbanization has had little impact on the villages. The result has been the segmentation of Liberian society into two coexisting subsystems—traditional-rural and modern-urban. (Liberia - People | Britannica)

Festivals, Holidays, and Music

The *World Atlas* describes popular festivals celebrated in the nation:

> Numerous activities geared towards the young generation including live performances, games, and contests take place during the festival which sees thousands of children from all over Liberia come together.

An important national holiday in the country is Independence Day which is observed each year on July 26th. Liberia also observes religious holidays including Christmas, Easter, and Eid al Fitr. The country has a close relationship with the United States as it was established during the repatriation of slaves in the 19th Century. A testament of the close relationship shared between the two countries is the observation of "Thanksgiving Day in Liberia." The observation of the holiday is provided for by law and is observed on November 4th each year.

From its founding until today, Liberia maintains a close cultural bond with the United States (The Culture Of Liberia - WorldAtlas). A popular music style is called "highlife music, a blend of western and local music styles that developed in the mid-twentieth century. Hip-hop is especially enjoyed by Liberia's youth. This music genre "borrows heavily from local languages and is locally known as 'Hipco.'" Popular performers use Hipco "as a tool of activism to criticize government policies and moral decay in society. However, those residing in the country's rural regions enjoy traditional music" ("The Culture Of Liberia" - WorldAtlas).

Natural Resources

According to *Britannica.com*:

> Agriculture is the leading sector of the economy. About half the land area is suitable for cultivation, though a small percentage is actually cultivated. Commercial farms are often operated by foreigners. Traditional farms, which comprise the largest number, are usually cultivated by slash-and-burn methods.

The climate supports rubber production that remains in operation since 1926, when the Firestone Tire and Rubber Company in the U.S. was given a concession for "rubber cultivation…by far the country's most valuable commercial crop" (*Britannia.com*). Deep-sea fishing is another source of income. Women comprise two-fifths of the workforce, including agriculture.

Liberia has abundant natural resources, including iron ore, diamonds, lead, gold, manganese, and others. War damage in the late twentieth century and UN sanctions until 2007 to prevent the commercialization of "blood diamonds" for terrorist weapons crippled Liberia's economy, but it is slowly being revived. Hydroelectric power has significant potential following severe damage to the country's infrastructure during the civil war era. The tourist trade weakened during the civil wars, but several popular sites in Liberia are attracting a growing number of visitors.

The U.S. dollar was previously the sole legitimate currency in Liberia. Now, however, the Central Bank of Liberia issues the Liberian dollar.

Culture

Health and medical services, while not strong to begin with, were disrupted and damaged during the civil wars. HIV/AIDS is a growing concern for Liberia, like other regional countries. Education faltered as families fled war-torn regions – often after losing one or more members to the conflicts.

According to *Britannica.com*, traditional and Western lifestyles coexist, although traditional values influence Western customs. Rural areas prefer traditional music, dance, and dress. "Schools instruct students in the legends, traditions, songs, arts, and crafts of African culture, and the government promotes African culture through such agencies as the National Museum in Monrovia, the Tubman Center for African Culture in Robertsport, and the National Cultural Center in Kendeja, which exhibits architecture of the 16 ethnic groups of Liberia. Mask making is an artistic pursuit that is also related to the social structure of some ethnic groups."

Liberia's American heritage remains in full force today. In part, connections to the U.S. economy keeps the native Liberians from embracing their traditional identity and Liberian lifestyle due to the glittery temptations of Western ideologies, economies, and entertainments. The American and European trade agreements with Liberia and financial support since its founding and during its development have prevented African residents from exploring and following their traditional lifestyle and values. Although potentially well intended, the U.S. controls placed on Liberia's path to progress, and organic self-realization have kept our nation from becoming self-reliant by utilizing our natural resources and innate skills of our people.

> Liberia, the land of the free, is unique in several aspects. It is a land of many stories with several of them untold. It is a land of hope and great opportunities ... but it is also a land of pain, poverty, and despair.
> ... Liberia has a literacy rate of just 60.8% for the entire population with the female literacy rate hovering around 56.8%. In other words, quality education which helps a lot in building strong economies, is something very lacking in Liberia today. Children of school-going age are often seen along the streets of major towns and cities hawking and petty trading. Most rural communities lack proper educational facilities. (*Africa and the World*, Major problems facing Liberia today (africaw.com)

Ill-equipped medical facilities and lack of safe drinking water as well as sewage disposal contribute to Liberia's health woes. Weak governance, corruption, dependence on foreign aid, and epidemics of HIV/AIDS and Ebola have crippled Liberia's infrastructure in the sectors of health, education, and finances. The next generation of youth are ill prepared to tackle the legacy of problems and challenges that continue to damage our nation and keep it from healing and prospering. Lack of support for issues related to transportation, agriculture, deforestation, and ocean pollution keep a chokehold on Liberia to prevent it from becoming independent of foreign support and fully developing our national resources. Liberian residents are unable to obtain adequate employment to support a viable lifestyle, and many professionals who are hired to help our country survive and thrive are undereducated or misled by superstition and greed for Western opulence.

Families are broken by divorce or having babies without a secure marital structure. Domestic violence against women and minorities remains a critical concern. Children raised without the benefit of their elders' wisdom and guidance fail to adjust to a healthy mindset of ethical and moral norms.

Still, the Liberian people in general want a better life, and many are willing to work for it. We need resolute, visionary leaders who will put our nation's needs ahead of their own. The following chapter will examine the ways in which Liberia can begin to embrace a more positive and productive approach to repairing our wounds from the past to build a successful future.

Chapter 7
The Way Forward

Liberia's Government must be headed by a leader that puts the needs of our nation ahead of international interests or personal gain or somebody. Liberia has already lost so much but has far more to gain with the guidance and support of responsible leadership. The country's primary goals are as follow:

a) Set forth plans with built-in measures that will serve as platforms to establish an Agreement through a popular vote by the people of Liberia. The State – as a unique entity – is larger than the Government, and the Government serves as an agent of the State. A structured and citizen-approved Government is supposed to protect and seek the wellbeing of its citizens. Instead, unprepared or corrupt African government has instituted unsuitable leadership - the opposite objective that the government is pledged to uphold when is empowered.

b) Unite the country and change the mindset of today's residents. The original outlook was brought into Liberia by the pioneers of the ACS, including "Grab and Go." We must work diligently together to help Liberians to feel like a valuable and necessary part of their society and to behave as stakeholders. Our people should be helped to understand they do not need to leave Liberia to be successful or find contentment. Liberia's citizens must become aware of all the ways that they can be comfortable and fulfilled in our country.

c) Discourage foreigners – especially those who hold oversight roles - from bribing the infrastructure and abusing our citizens through deception and misconduct.

d) Develop a clear, organized, and success-oriented agenda for immediate implementation that will move Liberia in a series of phases toward long-term stability and success.

e) Establish a system to ensure that utilizes confidence building that will not hinder interrelationships between the public and the government.

f) Reduced corruption, people must be willing and able to take these steps:

- Expose corrupt activities and the associated risks.
- Hold the public sectors to standards of honesty, transparency, and accountability to facilitate public trust.
- Identify and remove or prevent dishonest practices in society through legal means.
- Ensure that public sector employees act in the public interest - not personal interest.
- Reduce poverty and encourage community and government engagements regularly to address these and related issues.
- Clear guidelines are needed to organize strategies for dealing with these critical issues in a timely manner. As we begin to deal comprehensively with core problems, we can encourage and support healthy reform.

Poverty, Government and Distrust

Liberians are peaceful and loving people. But the government has not implemented any real poverty reduction strategies to help alleviate widespread poverty and its attendant problems of social inequities, crime, and hopelessness. The result has been a growing level of distrust and disrespect within the population, especially without the means or a plan to escape generational poverty.

Lacking education and equal job opportunities, people tend to form friendships and professional associations based on how they stand to benefit from those relationships, regardless of the objectivity of that situation. Then, if and when the opportunity passes or ends, they will turn against their Liberian brothers and sisters once there is nothing to benefit or be gained. To solve this problem, there should be government programs to reduce poverty to a reasonable level and enforce a liberalization policy while also welcoming our foreign friends for the sake of Liberia's growth and wellbeing.

In developed countries, there are strong policies that foster mutual respect and cooperation for enjoying a quality standard of living and maintaining peaceful relations with others. Citizens are urged to love each other and their country. In Liberia, due to legal issues, everyone tries to protect their personal space to avoid intruders. Poverty in our midst causes us to hate each other and befriend those who have what we need regardless of whether or not they are Liberian. It is neither normal nor intentional that we hate each other as fellow citizens. That is why we keep looking forward to a government that will provide necessary programs to bond us as a nation and as a people such that we can work together and help each other when in need.

A good team with a bad idea is better than a bad team with a good idea.

From 1822 to 2022, leaders in Liberia have accepted the model of "a good idea with a bad team" strategy. Americo-Liberians between 1822 to 1980 and Indigenous people since 1980 to the present have formed bad teams. A "bad team" understands exactly what is good and befitting for the nation but refuses to seek knowledge and yield to advice. Instead, these teams will create the wrong mindset and promote it throughout the country for personal gain. An example is the Congress for Democratic Change (CDC) in Liberia, which promised good ideas like "I will encourage the War Crime Court upon winning the election." CDC fell short after winning the General Election because of its nature as a bad team.

"A good team with a bad idea" is likely to seek or adopt good ideas and yield to wise counsel. A "good team" government should seek knowledge by means of consultation for the following purposes:

A) Provide jobs to build and renovate cities
B) Build express lanes with exits connecting all counties and neighboring countries
C) Stabilize electricity – A responsible government must rebuild a hydro-system to boost the Liberia economic throughout the Country. Retain the old hydro for few communities that it can contain reasonably.
D) Standardize the airport and seaport – Improvement within these sectors will also provide a huge boost to the Liberian economic.
E) Preserve traditions and cultures of various tribes in museums
F) Standardize medical facilities
G) Update and improve education – No child left behind program, a good educational policy and implementations process is a promising future for Liberia as well. Liberians are smart and willing to learn but yet anxious for opportunities.

Voting and Appointments

The Election Commission and the court system must have reasonable criteria set forth as a means for helping the Liberian people to vet contestants before elections or appointments. How can you have a Truth & Reconciliation Commission (TRC) indicted person qualified to contest the Legislature, Senate, or appointed positions? How can you have a person appointed to a position of trust when s/he has a proven tainted character?

To move our country forward, we must be able to set forth a workable system with a strong commitment to change society and create a merit system. The Executive Branch, Lawyers, judges and

Legislators must also have monitoring system of assets. They should declare assets after winning election/s or when appointed. This will help direct and control resources to sectors correctly. A regular expenditure audit routing must be done and recommendation shall be implemented by a responsible government to ensure resources are use for its intended purposes.

Freedom of the Press

Press Freedom must be encouraged to enable everyone to express themselves. In so doing, we can find better ways to address those concerns in the interests of the Liberian people as they relate to our day-to-day activities.

Frequent briefing of the Liberian people is essential to any government since they are the employer.

*****

STEP-BY-STEP ROAD MAP TO TRUE INDEPENDENT OF LIBERIA

1. Unification for all Liberians (Current - Priority)
2. Liberalization policy is Key to uplifting Liberians out of Poverty.
3. Build Standard Prisons to serve as deterrence and help bring out the good from within our Brothers, Sisters and foreign friends:

    Many people involved in criminal activities are responded to with impunity in Liberia due to the following reasons.

    *   Culture. In Africa, there is a belief system that is changing very slowly. A common principle is that a family bears a child, but it is the responsibility of the entire town to raise that child. In a sense, the child belongs to the town. To punish a child, everyone believes it will hunt them or they may become enemies of their town. For change to come that leads to fair and equitable

law enforcement, please read point number 2 below.

* Traditions. To change a pattern of thought, action, or behavior (such as a religious practice or a social custom of the people of Liberia), it is difficult but possible by means of sincere leadership and education. Society must support everyone with open minds, clean hands, and sincerity to make things right in the community.

NOTE: Liberians have a wait-and-see test to evaluate leaders' sincerity in a desire to change society. This method has worked for many regimes, including that of George Weah and his first term evaluation result, which caused him serious trouble.

* Cartel. A cartel is a combination of political groups for common action. In a society such as Liberia, politicians have always created coalitions to win elections, since it is a multi-party country. The Constitution also provides that a party must win with 50+1 percent majority to emerge the winner. This constitutional mandate gave rise to coalitions. It becomes difficult for a winning party to deliver to his/her employers, i.e., the Liberian people, because he or she usually makes numerous promises to other parties to help during the election process. As when forming a coalition, there is a standard for give and take.

4. Border Control to avoid economic leakages on land, air and sea – This will help keep the country safe:

NOTE: Immigration or joint security will need to control the inflow and outflow of large numbers of people and goods into Liberia to ensure this benefit is given only to those in need, mainly Liberians as beneficiary. It has been observed that some groups of people make large movements within the sub-region wherever there is a huge benefit within a particular Country. These Economic Movements within the sub-region is creating a high cost that forces assistance programs expenditures to skyrocket and most times leads to Program failure since the expenditures will by far exceed the income.

This kind of assistance programs cause and cost most developed countries to tighten immigration to avoid huge unskilled Foreigner/s to move there to take away such offers from their vulnerable people..

5. Improved Social Security for retirement
6. Encourage merit system and great incentives
7. Encourage community participation in national issues
8. Empower citizens to be self sufficient

   For community leaders, country leaders, and business professionals and government arms that implement projects to be held accountable in court for their roles by the Liberian People through their government, there must be a code of conduct, and the president must relinquish some authority to them without interference except by court orders for accountabilities based on audit or committee report/s

9. Reduce poverty aggressively
10. Zero hunger
11. Good health care and wellbeing
12. Quality education – No Child Left Behind Program
13. Gender equality
14. Clean water and sanitation
15. Affordable and clean energy
16. Decent work and economic growth: Not economic growth without development
17. Industrialize innovation and infrastructure
18. Reduce inequalities
19. Sustainable cities and communities:

Most Vulnerable and Mental Health Issues within Liberia:

Our brothers and sisters who are borne deform or naturally needs societal help because of vulnerabilities and those who have chosen to be on the streets smoking, injecting, and inhaling toxic chemicals have become a national problem, and it is every sober Liberian's responsibility to help them. We need to evaluate each situation on a case-by-case basis regardless of the many different reasons for their actions. If we do nothing, society suffers the consequences as victims of theft or robbery.

We will need to invest in a huge consultancy, seeking solutions, such as proposals and funding to help our citizens. We must remove them from the streets and graveyards to clean up our cities and create safe movements within various communities mainly for our sisters and Mothers who must be home very early every day to avoid harassment or risk of being rape. Specialized doctors should examine suspicious-looking persons who are street smoking, injecting, and inhaling dangerous substances to determine who goes to rehab or prison, or to keep them within government sponsored program homes under 24/7 supervision, thus creating meaningful employment for capable Liberians.

Substance – (Drug) User/s

Liberians must stop and refrain from naming our vulnerable brothers and sister as Zongo with a common understand which could mean "bad guys". Naming them as Zongo could cause them to unite, withdraw in a hateful form and focus their target group for survivor.

Initial Therapeutic treatment begins with:

1. Respecting vulnerable people and calling them by name/s –
2. Listening to them
3. Providing Care in all aspect (health, clothing, housing, food, etc etc), Some of them felt left out of the National Cake and neglected so they chose a ghetto or different life style from normal.

This process will require specialized doctors, all forms of military forces, law enforcement officers, and immigration authorities to facilitate Liberians through legislative action to succeed. These costly programs are essential to help reduce crime restrict large crowds from the public streets in Liberia.

To succeed in promoting programs to control substance abuse and clear our communities to make then safer for the Liberian people – mainly for our mothers and sisters – we may need to do the following:

- Recruit, hire, and retain medical professionals and social workers along with volunteers.
- Examine all types of substance users and recommend possible candidates for rehab.
- Suggest treatment and hospitals to partner both within and outside of Liberia:
- Train candidates capable of employment with others monitored 24/7 by staff.

Military and para-military support:

- Contain those who accept results after examination but refuse to enroll within the program by being monitored in daily activities.
- Contain those who refuse both results and enrollment within the program and want to live in denial yet move about freely and continue to instill fear in the communities.
- Help enforce doctors', psychiatrists', and social worker's recommendations for betterment of our brothers and sisters who choose that lifestyle.

Liberia needs to seek much more research and deploy technologies to fully achieve this GOAL.

Advantages to helping our Liberian brothers and sisters:

1. Reduce crime
2. Create jobs

3. Help and enable those vulnerable, substance injectors or mental health people discover or spot a gift within themselves to aid them transition when necessary to become better citizen/s.

4. Help Liberians develop the love for our country and fellow human beings by caring for themselves and contributing to a healthy and productive society.

20. Responsible consumption and production

21. Climate action

22. Life below water: Clean Liberia water

23. Life on land: Animals must survive with our help

24. Peace, justice, and strong institutions
    NOTE: Regardless of the situation, leadership makes the difference. Remember, a good team with a bad idea is better than a bad team with a good idea. A good team will always seek knowledge to do the right thing, but a bad team will manipulate the people for personal gain, thus creating a cartel of pride dominants.
    Liberians will know you because of the Note in #2.
    Liberians deserve better and need a good leader who is selfless and aware of the Liberians' wait-and-see methods of evaluations to gain their trust.
    A leader's selflessness and consciousness will be depicted within various developments and all aspects of society as well as seen in every county.

25. Partnership for the Goals: our foreign friends/allies
    —Include graphic demonstrations as well for easy understanding
    a. System builds with technology for all sectors of governments to solve, regulate, and gather data as quick as possible when necessary
    b. Whistleblowers protection and awards within every aspect of government

26. I believe the Military and Paramilitary institutions are re-

sponsible to a large extent to provide protection for the citizens of Liberia.

27. Another way the government can sincerely fight crime around the country is to provide budgetary allotments for other institutions, such as the Inter-Faith Council of Liberia and the Council of Churches of Liberia as well. This will create huge independence within each religious practicing group to become a Patriot and avoid being influenced by any wealthy member/s. This method will help fight crime within every community because almost everyone is a part of a religious group.

28. Once government makes appropriation for all religious groups, they automatically serve their country as a whistleblower against any crimes that have the potential of disturbing a community and to professionally report activities that will be investigated in a timely and covert manner:

29. Suspicious activities, large donations, huge lifestyle changes, huge influence on others and any unwholesome acts, etc.

30. A committee to swiftly investigate allegations against government officials and/or staff to improve conduct and productivity

31. Encourage CC Camera in public places

Strategy to Engage Executives

The President has the absolute authority to ensure that the resulting "roadmap" be implemented by a robust monitoring process:

The Dean of Cabinet, which is the Minister of Foreign Affairs, has delicate responsibilities because of two major reasons:

1) Responsibility to ensure there is a quarterly cabinet meeting for ministries and autonomous agencies in which everyone will be regularly monitored and supervised. This will enable the Dean to brief the president for decision making. A retreat could be held once a year in a designated venue.

A) At the onset of a responsible government after election,

each ministry and autonomous agency must submit a work plan with a budget.

B) By this the Dean will be kept informed of all Ministry and agency priorities. He/she will determine whether a deficiency in a particular sector is the result of a budget shortfall or mismanagement by allowing auditors to probe the financial matters.

Example:

Recently, the Robert International Airport Authority has caused two major Airlines to be delayed in landing due to locked electricity. Those aircraft had to reroute to Sierra Leone for landing, thus promising not to return to Liberia unless the situation is improved upon. It is important to launch an immediate audit probe to ascertain what went wrong. Is the funding insufficient or misused? Upon this determination, the president will now be brief by the head of the cabinet regarding the situation and make suggestions to remedy the problem. One of the solutions is, if it is due to locked funding, we turn to the head of the cabinet.

On Wednesday, April 27, 2022, Brussels Airlines rerouted flight SN241 to Freetown (FNA), Sierra Leone, after the Airbus A330-300 registered OO-SFC suddenly aborted landing at Monrovia's Robert International Airport (RIA), Liberia, due to a power outage at the airport and on the runway. Another situation was that Royal Air Maroc was compelled to abort landing at RIA due to dark runways. The flight attempted landing several times by using the navigation system but was unsuccessful. Royal Air Maroc was forced to divert to Sierra Leone. The inability of the flight landing at RIA left several passengers who were to board the flight stranded at the Airport. Air France, Vice President for Africa, Mr. Jean-Marc Pouchol, met with Liberia Minister of Transport, Mr. Charles De Gaulle. "Based on the economic performance," Air France has decided to suspend its flight to Monrovia, Liberia, as of April 2022.

(https://www.aviation24.be/airlines/lufthansa-group/brussels-airlines/suspends-flights-to-monrovia-liberia/)

Brussels Airlines is forced to cancel flights between Brussels Airport, Belgium, and Monrovia Airport, Liberia, until further notice. In a statement to Liberian news media, the Belgian airline explained it had to take the drastic measure as the airport lacks proper approach and landing systems in accordance with the airline's operating procedures and international aviation law.

Frontpage Africa knows that the ICAO gave Liberia three months' time to repair the damaged equipment, including the navigation systems and the Instrument Landing System (ILS) Localizer at the airport of Monrovia.

During a "grace period" of three months, Brussels Airlines was still able to operate flights toward the country but has now informed the airport authorities that it no longer can continue to risk its aircraft and flout Belgian aviation laws.

The airport also faces other problems as on 27 April, Brussels Airlines had to turn back to Freetown, Sierra Leone, over a power outage at the airport of Monrovia.

Reporters have been told that a complete renovation to fix all the problems would cost around $20 million.

Today's flight SN241 toward Monrovia via Freetown has been cancelled. The airline confirmed to ***Aviation24.be*** that it will operate today's flight to Freetown in combination with Abidjan, Côte d'Ivoire, and Cotonou, Benin, as SN1233 with an extra crew.

(Source: Liberia: SN Brussels Cancels Flights to Monrovia over Safety Concerns at the Roberts International Airport)

The Foreign Minister is responsible for creating and maintaining a good relationship with regional and international partners and know their strength in terms of assistance and when Liberia can reciprocate. Having understood everything surrounding the airport, we must now determine whether to involve regional or international partner/s. A regional partner could help with electricity from Côte d'Ivoire, a country sharing borders with Liberia.

These situations are untenable in efforts to build and sustain mutually beneficial international partnerships. Contributing factors must be addressed and resolved for Liberia to become a respected and trustworthy international partner with these and other nations who share common goals and interests.

*****

Goal: Unification

Liberia Civil War:

Politicians have created a severe problem among the tribes of Liberia, thus resulting in the fourteen-year civil war. Warlords were established to carry out the unethical politicians' dirty work but soon lost control over these regional chieftains.

Since the Civil War ended, the various tribes have been accused and targeted by each other's for the loss of relatives and wealth within their settlements. Because of this fear, many tribes still vote for corrupt politicians over good politicians hoping for system changed and decent Unification packaged that will build TRUST amongst them . Because of fear amidst the Tribes, they rather vote unscrupulous warlords and crooks of their kind, to raise a false front and please them, so they stand up for them in case of attack or conflict from another tribes. These representatives sent a warfare strength signal to other tribes.

An effective leadership needs to disarm these tribes by Political, Social, and Economic FEAR means to achieve a healthy, citizen-centric balance in Liberia. When the tribes build trust in their leadership for protection and stronger unification programs, they will gradually disarm themselves and begin to vote for competent leaders, thus helping to move the country forward in a positive direction.

Land Disputes:

Land disputes have taken many lives and are causing people to lose money. The problem stems from limited land space in the midst of a rapidly growing population with limited knowledge to raise and use unlimited resources, thus resulting in fear for tribes to accommodate each other's.

Two Major Factors Causing Land Disputes:

1. Some groups of people are presumed denied to form part of a settlement or a county.
2. Crooks sell land to multiple buyers, resulting in conflict and lost funds without legal ramifications.

Suggestion for Land Disputes and Tribal Conflict as Part of Unification Program:

1. Responsible leadership is KEY to resolving land disputes in Liberia.
2. Technology must be implemented to ensure security and ownership of land are guaranteed.
3. Skyscrapers must be constructed as a means of rebuilding the cities to accommodate millions of residents in smaller apartments and homes. Development with accurate census taken and many other factors are key for Liberia resolving land disputes. Liberians should be given choices to live in any part of their country at will without obstacles like bad roads, damaged vehicles, unnecessary delays, security checkpoints, etc. This will also de-tribalize the country and disarm citizens of their fear of securing land space due to size. The process of constructing and maintaining cities will create stable and long-term jobs.
4. Immigration must be robust and account for almost everyone.

When these and similar measures are instituted, Liberia will grow stronger and provide a secure, wholesome, and fruitful environment for its citizenships and the future.

Reduce Poverty Aggressively:

The Weah-led government won the 2017 election with the promise of lifting Liberians from acute poverty. This message resonated with the citizens because George Weah is from a slum community. His experience from this type of background could encourage him to understand the citizens' pains and plight to do exactly that which he had promised.

Two years after the election, the George Weah government decided to harmonize civil servants' salaries.

The government pronounced its intention to massively reduce disparities in the public sector pay. It is just practical to launch a salary harmonization exercise to address the biases and re-establishment of equity in the pay structures, which will ultimately lead to salary reductions affecting over 100 spending agencies of government. After the harmonization, the reality was directly opposite to their pronounced intent, like getting rid of biases within the salary structures. Poverty increased massively, creating a wide gap that is resulting in a class system. This harmonization places many people in acute poverty that is contrary to his campaign promises.

*****

Reference below: *Liberia Observer* (Hannah N. Geterminah, September 13, 2019)

Liberia: GOL Harmonization Affects 66,538 Employees

Facebook Twitter WhatsApp Flipboard LinkedIn Reddit Email Share

13 SEPTEMBER 2019
Liberian Observer (Monrovia)
By Hannah N. Geterminah

The government's harmonization process has affected 66,538 employees from various ministries, agencies, and local authorities.

Del-Francis Wreh, executive director for Macroeconomic Policy Analysis Center at the Ministry of Finance and Development

Planning (MFDP), made the disclosure on Thursday, September 12, 2019 at the Ministry of Information regular press briefing in Monrovia.

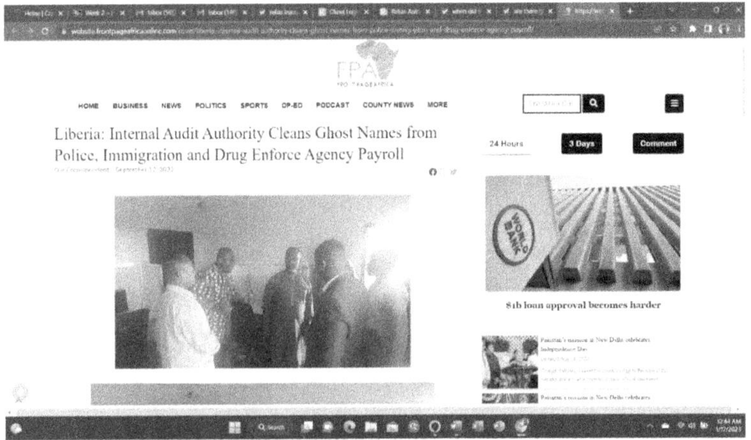

Chapter Eight
About the Author

My parents were both Loma from Lofa County in Liberia. I was born to Mr. and Mrs. Dayrell in Liberia. My racial background and roots are from Lofa County, Liberia, in West Africa, from a small ethnic and marginalized community known as the Loma people. The Loma ethnic group is predominantly found in Liberia and Guinea and is estimated to be approximately 400,000 in the two countries.

Loma Ethnic Group in Liberia

As members of the Loma ethnic community, we are part of the sixteen tribal groupings that constitute the Liberian population. Through my parents and grandparents, I have learned that the Loma people were among the last ethnic groups in Liberia to submit to colonial rule as they valued and treasured their independence and were leading to fight to protect our culture and indigenous political system. Unfortunately, due to the resistance and defiance to bow down to the colonial administration, the Loma ethnic groups were dealt a heavy blow intended to dismantle them by eradicating their elaborate and deeply entrenched cultural institutions and political systems (Torino et al., 2018). However, despite the heavy and sustained attacks toward the dismantling of the Loma ethnics by the colonial administration and the successive regimes, we have stood firm to protect our cultural identity, traditions, ancestry, religion, and language in whatever part of the world that we migrate to in search of greener pastures.

My Loma ethnic group comprised predominantly farmers as they used the rainforest climate to plant rice and other crops. They practiced swidden agriculture. The Loma people inhabited areas rich in iron ore, and they consequently used iron as a form of currency. The Loma people in Liberia stood out among the ethnic groups due to their rich cultural identity. Secret societies, frequent warfare, and matrilateral cross-cousin marriage are also part of the cultural identity of my Loma people (Bedert, 2017).

The Poros society was a secret society for men while the Soros were the female equivalent in the Loma ethnic group. A secret society in the cultural context relates to an organization where members swear a secrecy oath about their activities. The establishment of multi-ethnic chiefdoms and fragmented governments based on territory and kinship were prominent features in my Loma ethnic group. Mande is the main language spoken by the Loma ethnic group in Liberia.

Education

March 31th, 2023 Graduate of the Capella University: MS in Human Services

- Areas of Study: Leadership and Organizational Management
- Capella University, United States of America

1998 to 2006

- Bachelor of Arts, Accounting: Cum Laude
- University of Liberia, Monrovia, Liberia

1996 to 1998

- AA Degree in Accounting
- College of West Africa, Program of Business, Monrovia, Liberia

1993 to 1994

- High School Diploma and WAEC Certificate Division 1

Current Employment

October 2021 to Present   Step by Step, Inc., King of Prussia,
                                 1012 W. 9th Ave., Suite 125, King
                                 of Prussia, PA 19406

Previous Employment:

April 2014 to March 2015:

Risk Manager
First International Bank (Liberia) Ltd.
Monrovia, Liberia

Responsibilities:
As a Risk Manager, or Risk Assessment Manager, I was responsible
for determining the types of risks that could affect workplace financial
health, legal compliance, or reputation. My duties included communi-
cating with company leadership personnel, Department Managers, or
legal staff, reviewing operational procedures, employee data, or mar-
ket trends and presenting findings to upper management personnel
and reporting quarterly to the Board.

*****

December 2010 to December 2011:

General Ledger Accountant
Total Liberia Inc.

Responsibilities:
My work was to support budgeting and forecasting. Entering financial
data such as accruals, deferrals, reclassifications, and interdepartmen-
tal entries into the ledger on a monthly basis, as well as preparing reports. Performing account analysis to ensure that journal entries and
balances are correct.

*****

January 2012 to March 2014:

Audit Manager
First International Bank (Liberia) Ltd.

Responsibilities:
As Audit Manager, it was my responsibility to oversee internal operating controls, processes, and practices. I could also recommend changes and enhancements to existing policies and controls to make sure they are current, adequate, functional, and utilized in accordance with standards established by the government and the company. As Audit Manager, I managed a team of junior auditors/accountants, reviewing their works and providing guidance. I submitted reports to top management and quarterly to the Board.

*****

2008 to 2010:

Audit Senior 111
VOSCON INC. Auditing Firm
Buchanan Street, Monrovia Liberia

*****

2005 to 2008:

Accountant
International Republican Institute (IRI/LIBERIA)
40 Carey Street Monrovia, Liberia:
Supervisor: Monte McMurchy, Program Director
Email: montemcmurchy@sympatico.ca

*****

Professional Skills
- Ability to Build Team Spirit
- Effective Supervisory Skills
- Computer Literacy (Microsoft Word, Excel, PowerPoint)
- High Concentration to Job Details, Problem Solving
- Communication Skill in English (Verbal and non-verbal)
- Trustworthiness and Good Decision Making Skill

*****

Reference Notes

(Attribute Table Field DescriptionsISO3 - International Organization for Standardization 3-digit country code ADM0_NAME - Administration level zero identification / name ADM1_NAME - Administration level one identification / name ADM2_NAME - Administration level two identification / name - Name of religious institution TYPE - Classification in the geodatabase (type of institution) CITY - City location available SPA_ACC - Spatial accuracy of site location (1 – high, 2 – medium, 3 – low) COMMENTS - Comments or notes regarding the religious institution SOURCE_DT - Source one creation date SOURCE - Source one SOURCE2_DT - Source two creation date SOURCE2 - Source two Collection The feature class was generated utilizing data from OpenStreetMap, Wikimapia, GeoNames and other sources. OpenStreetMap is a free worldwide map, created by crowdsourcing. Wikimapia is open-content mapping focused on gathering all geographical objects in the world. GeoNames is a geographical places database maintained and edited by an online community. Consistent naming conventions for geographic locations were attempted but name variants may exist, which can include historical or less widespread interpretations. The data included herein have not been derived from a registered survey and should be considered approximate unless otherwise defined. While rigorous steps have been taken to ensure the quality of each dataset, DigitalGlobe is not responsible for the accuracy and completeness of data compiled from outside sources. Metadata information was collected form U.S. Department of State publications as well as news media articles. Sources (HGIS) "Cathedral of St. Therese of The Child Jesus." GCatholic. July 2014. Accessed October 7, 2014. http://www.gcatholic.org.DigitalGlobe, "DigitalGlobe Imagery Archive." Accessed October 01, 2014. GeoNames, "Liberia." September 23, 2014. Accessed October 01, 2014. http://www.geonames.org.Google, September 2014. Accessed October 01, 2014. www.google.com.OpenStreetMap, "Liberia." September 2014. Accessed October 01, 2014. http://www.openstreetmap.org.Wikimapia, "Liberia." September 2014. Accessed October 01, 2014. http://wikimapia.org.Sources (Metadata)Baden, Joel, and Candida Moss. "Ebola Is Not God's Wrath: Religious leaders are perpetuating dangerous, dehumanizing beliefs about sin and disease." Slate. August 20, 2014. Accessed October 01, 2014. http://www.slate.com. "Country Profile: Liberia."

Soudan Interior Mission. January 01, 2014. Accessed October 01, 2014. http://www.sim.org. "Education System in Liberia." Classbase. January 01, 2012. Accessed October 01, 2014. http://www.classbase.com. "Liberia 2005 International Religious Freedom Report." United States Department of State: Bureau of Democracy, Human Rights, and Labor. January 01, 2005. Accessed October 01, 2014. http://www.state.gov. "Liberia 2012 International Religious Freedom Report." United States Department of State: Bureau of Democracy, Human Rights, and Labor. January 01, 2005. Accessed October 01, 2014. http://www.state.gov. "Liberia 2014 International Religious Freedom Report." United States Department of State. January 01, 2014. Accessed October 01, 2014. (http://www.state.gov. Liberia Religious Institutions | ArcGIS Hub)

www.ingramcontent.com/pod-product-compliance
Lightning Source LLC
Chambersburg PA
CBHW061352140726
47997CB00003B/1173